D0807154

Serigne Mara Diakhate

Talking Wolof
With
Da' African Village:

A Speaker's Guide to Senegal/West Africa

By

Serigne Mara Diakhate

Copyright © 2013 Serigne Mara Diakhate

International All Rights Reserved

ISBN-13: 978-0615882161

Book cover design, editor, and English language consultant: Pamela Norris

This book was printed in the United States of America.

To order more copies of this book, contact:
Da' African Village
Website: www.daafricanvillage.com
Email: daafricanvillage@gmail.com
Office: (877) 203-5089

DEDICATION

This book is dedicated to my entire family. You are the force that drives me to achieve great things. May God bless your journey even more than mine.

CONTENTS

ACKNOWLEDGMENTS

First and foremost I want to thank God for blessing me with the gift of being a tour guide, tour operator, entrepreneur, and the opportunity to share my gift with the world. I believe that God gives everyone a special mission to accomplish in his or her lifetime, and I am grateful that God has entrusted me with such a special mission.

I want to acknowledge the people of America. For without your openness to learn and embrace new cultures, this book may not have been born. Thank you for allowing me to be the one to guide you to the bridge to Senegal.

Thanks to the Diakhate and Sane family for your undying support and believing in my career. I would also like to thank Jo Keita (Nubian Tours), Robin Thorne, The Agape Spiritual Church in Los Angeles, Ibrahima Keith Holt, Fallou Mboup, Joy Day, Laye Thiam (Timbuk Tours, New Jersey), and Salif Badiane (African Connection Tours)

A special thanks to Pamela Norris for your undying support, time, energy, and knowledge to make this book possible.

MAPS

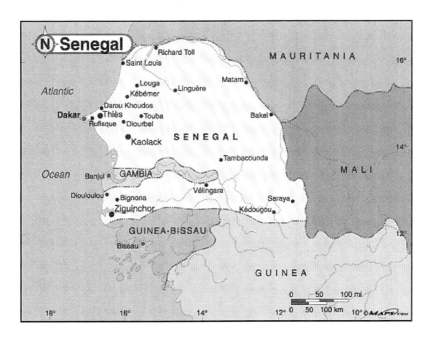

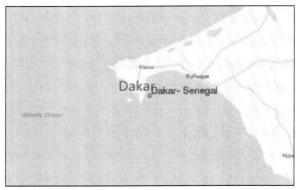

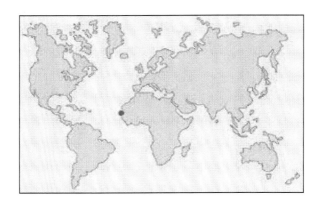

How To Use This Book

Senegal is located in the Western region of Africa stretching out into the Atlantic Ocean at the meeting point of Europe, Africa, and the Americas. The official language of Senegal is French and the national language is Wolof. Many natives of Senegal speak both French and Wolof. Wolof is primarily a spoken language with many dialects and not often used in written form.

This book is designed to serve as a guide to bridge the English language with Wolof. This book is not to be used as a dictionary. The spelling of Wolof words used in this book is for pronunciation purposes only. The words are modified phonetically for the English language speaker. For example, the Wolof word m*ungfa* is spelled *moongfa* to fit the phonetic sound/spelling of the English language. This book is written for people to learn speak basic conversational Wolof, and will definitely be a valuable tool for tourist traveling to Senegal. So, pick up the book and start "Talking Wolof."

"The Bridge Of Togetherness"

1. Greetings and Responses

Peace be unto you ....*Salamaleikum*

Peace be unto you to ....*Maleikumsalam*

How are you? .... *Nagadef*

I am fine .... *Magifeerek*

Good morning .... *Jama nga fanaan*

Good morning .... *Jama rek*

Good afternoon .... *Jama nga endu*

Good afternoon .... *Jama rek*

Good evening .... Jama nga endu

Good evening .... *Jama rek*

How are your families? .... *Naka seen wa kerr?*

They are ok (they are there) .... *Nyoongfa*

How is your family? .... *Naka sa wa kerr?*

They are ok .... *Nyoongfa*

How are the children? .... *Naka haleyi?*

They are ok .... *Nyoongfa*

How is your husband? .... *Naka sa jekerr?*

He is ok .... *Moongfa*

How is your wife? .... *Naka sa jabarr?*

She is ok .... *Moongfa*

How is your friend? .... *Naka sa haritt?*

He/she is ok .... *Moongfa*

How is your elder brother/sister? .... *Naka sa mack?*

He/she is ok .... *Moongfa*

How is your younger brother/sister? .... *Naka sa raka?*

He/she is ok .... *Moongfa*

How is work? .... *Naka leegay bee?*

It is ok (Thanks to God) .... *Saunta yallah*

Thank you .... *Jerrejeff*

You're welcomed .... *Nyoko boak*

Nice to meet you .... *Beygay nalla*

Let us see each other again .... *Nanu ghee sin te what*

In peace .... Chi jama, si jama

Grammatical Notes

There .... *Fa* (at the end of a word) for example, *Moongfa* always answers to the 3rd person singular, in this case *Moongfa* means *he is there, she is there*, or *it is there*.

2. Nouns/Pronouns

I	*Mann*
You	*Yow*
He/she	*Mōm*
We	*Nyun*
You	*Yen*
They	*Nyom*
My	*Suma*
Your	*Sa*
His/her	*Sa*
Our	*Sunyu*
Your	*Sen*
This	*Bee*
These	*Lola*
There	*Falah*
Here	*Fi*

3. Family Pronoun Combinations

Your friend..*Sa harrit*

Our friend...*Sunu harrit*

My child...*Suma dom*

Our mother...*Sunu yai*

This is my mother....................................*Ki moy suma yai*

This is my father.....................................*Ki moy suma bai*

Your father..Sa papa, *Sa bai*

His wife..*Jabar-ram*

Your wife..*Sa jabarr*

My elder brother.............................*Suma mak bo gorr*

My friend..*Suma harrit*

That woman...*Jagaen baleh*

This gun..*Fetel bee*

This fowl..*Ganar bee*

This house...*Kerr bee*

This room ....Neck bee

That bird..*Peecha baleh*

My name...*Suma turr*

My sense..*Suma hell*

My foot, my leg...*Suma tanka*

Nouns are formed by 'kat'

Farm .... *Bei*

Farmer .... *Bei kat*

Pass .... *Romba*

Pass by .... *Romba kat*

Wash .... *Fort*

Washer.. *Fort kat by jegaen*

Shave .... *Wat*

Barber .... *Wat kat*

Cook .... *Toga*

Chef .... Toga kat

4. Conjugation of Common Verbs

I am .... *Mann mai*

You are ....*Yow jai*

He/She is .... *Mōm moy*

We are .... *Nyun nyoi*

You are .... *Yen nyenla*

They are .... *Nyom joi*

I was .... *Mann nekona*

You were ....*Yow nekonga*

He/she was .... *Mōm nekon*

We were .... *Nyom nekonen*

You were ....*Yen nekongen*

They were .... *Nyom nekonen*

I will be .... *Mann dina neki*

You will be .... *Yow danga neki*

He/she will be .... *Mōm dina neki*

We will be .... *Nyoon dinen neki*

You will be .... *Yen dingen neki*

They will be .... *Nyom dinen neki*

I have .... *Mann am na*

You have .... *Yow am nga*

He/she has .... *Mōm amna*

We have .... *Nyom amnen*

You have .... *Yen amgen*

They have .... *Nyom amnen*

I had .... *Mann amo na*

You had .... *Yow amo nga*

He/she had .... *Mōm amo na*

We had .... *Nyom amo nen*

You had .... *Yen amo ngen*

They had .... *Nyom amo nen*

I will have .... *Mann dina am*

You will have .... *Yow dinga am*

He/she will have .... *Mōm dina am*

We will have .... *Nyom dinen am*

You will have .... *Yen dingen am*

They will have .... *Nyom dinan am*

I do .... *Mann def na*

You do .... *Yow def nga*

He/she does .... *Mōm def na*

We do .... *Nyun def nen*

They do .... *Nyom def nen*

I did .... *Mann defona*

You did .... *Yow defonga*

He/she did .... *Mōm defona*

We did .... *Nyun defonen*

You did .... *Yen defongen*

They did .... *Nyom defonen*

I will do .... *Mann dina def*

You will do .... *Yow deega def*

He/she will do .... *Mōm dina def*

We will do .... *Nyun dinen def*

You will do .... *Yen dingen def*

They will do .... *Nyom dinen def*

5. Imperative

Go..*Dem*

Go! ....*Demal*

Come...*Kai*

Come here...*Kai fi*

How; what ....*Naka*

Let's go...*An dem*

I will come..*Dina nyow*

Sit down..*Togal*

Sit on the floor..*Togal si soof*

Lie down on the floor ....*Teddal si soof?*

Stand up..*Tahauwal*

Run..*Daw*

Give this to him...*Joh ko li*

Give him food...*Joh ko nyam*

Give him the basket......................................*Joh ko panyeh*

6. Gender and Age

The gender is often shown by the addition: jeegan, gorr

Female...*Jeegan*

Male...*Gorr*

Older..Mack

Younger...Rack

7. Plurals

Plurals are formed by 'yi'

Man, men...*Gorr, gorryi*

Woman, women.....................................*Jegaen, jagaenyi*

Person, people..*Nit, nityi*

Child, children..*Halel, halelyi*

Child, children...*Guneh, guneyi*

Broom, brooms...*Baleh, baleyi*

8. Family Relationship

Grandmother..*Mom boo jeegan*

Grandfather...*Mom boo gorr*

Mother...*Yai*

Father..*Bai*

Aunt... *Yoom pine*

Uncle... *Nee jai*

Son...*Dom boo gorr*

Daughter...*Dom boo jeegan*

Child...*Hallay or Goonay*

Children.. *Hallayi or Guneyi*

Mother-in-law..*Gorro boo jeegan*

Father-in-law...*Gorro boo gorr*

Sister-in-law...*Gorro*

Brother-in-law.......................................*Gorro*

Older brother.................................*Mack boogorr*

Younger brother...........................*Rack boogorr*

Older Sister...............................*Mack boo jeegan*

Younger Sister.........................*Rack boo jeegan*

Cousin...................................*Domu nee jai*

Niece....................................*Jarbot boo jeegan*

Nephew...*Jarbot boo gorr*

Family...*Mbok*

Wife...*Jabarr*

Husband..*Jekerr*

Best friend...*Domu ndai*

Friend...*Harrit*

Neighbor...*Duhkando*

9. Family Related Questions and Answers

What is your name? ....   *No tudoo?*

My name is Pamela .... *Maghee tudoo, Pamela*

Pamela is my name .... *Pamela la tudoo*

Last name .... *Saunta*

What is your last name? ....*No saunta?*

Smith is my last name ....*Smith la saunta*

What is your wife's name?................ *Nu sa jabarr tudoo?*

What is your husband's name?......... *Nu sa jekerr tudoo?*

What is your sister's name?..........*Nu sa rack boo jeegan-tudoo?*

What is your brother's name?..........*Nu sa rack boo gorr-tudoo?*

Do you have children? .... *Am ga dom?*

Yes, I have children................................*Wow, am na dom*

No, I do not have children................ *Dedet, amu ma dom*

How many children do you have?..... *Nyata dom ga am?*

How many brothers do you have?.....*Nyata mack ga am?*

How many sisters do you have? ....*Nyata rack ga am?*

Are you married?.. *Yahghee say?*

Yes, I am married................................. *Waw maghee say*

No, I am not married........................... *Dedet, say you ma*

How long have you been married?...... *Nyata at gay say?*

I have been married for 2 years .... *Maghee say nyarr at?*

Where is your husband? ………....…………… *Ana sa jakerr?*

He is working... *Maghee leegay*

Where are your children? .... *Ana sa haleyi?*

They are at school.................................. *Nyunghee darra*

Where is your wife? .... *Ana sa jabarr?*

She is at home.. *Maghee kerr ga*

10. Common Verbs

Beat ……………………………………………………… *Dorr*

Be baptized…………………………………………… *Ngente*

Beg……………………………………………………… *Nyann*

Breath ……………………………………………………*Noki*

Broom……………………………………………… *Balleh*

Buy………………………………………………… *Jenda*

Close ……………………………………………… *Te-ch*

Come ……………………………………………… *Nyowal*

Cook ……………………………………………… *Toga*

Cut………………………………………………… *Doug*

Die……………………………………………..…… *Dae*

Dish ……………………………………………………*Ra-has*

Do ………………………………………………..… *Def*

Dream ……………………………………………… *Ghenta*

Drink ……………………………………………… *Nann*

Eat ……………………………………………..… *Lekah*

Farm ………………………………………………*Bei*

Fly …………………………………………………*Now*

Go back …………………………………….. *Delu ganaw*

Go home …………………………………….. *Nyeebi Kerr*

Hold ....*Tiyeh*

Hungry .... *Hif*

Jump .... Tub

Kill... *Rei*

Laugh .... *Reh*

Lay down.. *Tedda*

Learn... *Janga*

Lend me ....*Abaal ma*

Like.. *Buga*

Live... *Dunda*

Look.. *Kholl*

Make .... *Defar*

Pain.. *Mehti*

Pass.. *Romba*

Pay.. Fai

Pound.. *Woll*

Pray... *Julli*

Rest .... *Nopaleku*

Run .... *Daw*

See... *Ghiss*

Sell ....*Jai*

Send...*Yoni*

Sew ....*Nyaw*

Show ....*Woneh*

Sing... *Wei*

Sit .... *Torg*

Sweep...*Fompa*

Take a bath ....*Sangu*

Teach .... *Jangaleh*

Walk .... *Dŏh*

Walk fast .... *Wahu*

Want.. *Buga*

Wash.. *Forrt*

Wipe.. *Fompa*

Work .... *Leegay*

Write... *Bindah*

11. Location Related Questions & Answers

I am coming from the market
Manghee jogay marseh

I am going home
Manghee dem kerr

Where are you from?
Fan nga jogay?

I am from America
America la jogay

Where are you going?
Foi dem?

I am going to Senegal
Maghee dem Senegal

This is my first time in Senegal
Maghee dogga nyoh Senegal

I have come to Senegal before
Ñawanna Senegal

I am happy to be here
Maghee behgay nyoh Senegal

Do you have the internet?
Amga internet?

May I use your phone?
Aballma sa telephone?

Where do I buy a cell phone?
Fan lie jenday telephone?

Where do you live?
Foe duck?

A little outside the town
Si ganau dekuhbee tutee

Where is the bathroom?
Fan la toilet beenek?

Where is the market?
Fan la marseh beenek?

Where are you going?
Fan nga dem?

I am going to the market
Manghee dem marseh

I am going to the market
Da'may dem marseh

Where is the market?
Fan la marseh beenek?

Which market are you going to?
Ban marseh gendee dem?

I am intending to go to the beach
Da'may dem si gaych bee

I am intending to go to the hotel
Da'may dem si "hotel" bee

I am intending to go to Dakar
Da'may dem Dakar

I am going to the Teranga
Manghee dem Teranga Hotel

I am going to the garden
Manghee dem si tallboo ndau bee

What do you plant in your garden?
Loy jee si tallboo ndau bee?

I grow tomatoes, aubergine and cabbage
Jee na tamateh, batanse, ak supomay

The corn has not grown yet
Mbō-habee sa-hagool

I am going to the school
Manghee dem si darra bee

What do you learn?
Loy jang?

I am reading a European book
Terreh boo Tubab lai jang

I am going to Dakar
Manghee dem Dakar

My friend, when are you going back to England?
Suhma harrit, kan-nga deloo England?

This evening
Tye si ngone

How are you getting there?
Lu lie yoboo

The airplane will take me
Airplane bee mōmay yoboo

12. Useful Words and Phrases

Alone ……………………………………………...…… *Mahn Canna*

Ok …………………………………………………. *Bahna*

I am intending to go ……………………………. *Da'may dem*

I will go ……………………………………. *Deena dem*

Have a peaceful afternoon ………. *Naga am becheki jama*

I am going home for now............. *Manghee dema ngoom*

I am ok for now ……………………………... *Bahna ngoom*

I said I am tired .... Dema sona

I am sorry .... Ballma

13. Useful Questions

What did you say? .... *Lo wah?*

Do you smoke? .... Deega toh?

Do you have a cigarette? .... Amga cigarette?

Where is he?...*Ana mu?*

Where is your wife?....................................*Ana sa jabarr?*

Where is the lamp?....................................*Ana lampa bee?*

Where is your book?............................*Ana sa terreh bee?*

Where did you go?.. *For dem on?*

Where did you come from?...............................*For jogay*

Where did you pick it up?...........................*For ko forrae?*

What shall I do?..*Lan lai def?*

What do you say?...*Loh wah?*

What does he say?.. *Lan la wah?*

How do you do it?......................................*Naka nga defe?*

What shall I do with it?............................. *Lu ma koi def?*

What shall I do with it?........................ *Lu ma koi doyeh?*

14. Shopping

Meat

Meat .... *Yapa*

Pork .... *Yapi mbam*

Beef .... *Yapi nak*

Beef steak .... *Beeftake*

Fish .... *Jen*

Little dried fish .... *Tamba jen*

Big opened dried fish .... *Gedja*

Fruits and Vegetgables

Tomato .... *Tomateh*

Onion .... *Soblay*

Irish potato .... *Pombeetear*

Aubergine .... *Batanse*

Carrot .... *Carrot*

Groundnut .... *Gerrteh*

Roasted groundnut .... *Gerrteh charf*

Raw groundnut ....*Gerrteh haran*

Mango .... *Mahngo*

Orange .... *Orange*

Lime .... *Limong*

Salad .... *Salad*

Produce

Eggs .... *Nen*

Butter .... *Butter*

Milk .... *Māow*

Baking Goods

Sugar .... *Sukurr*

Flour .... *Farine*

Bread .... *Mburu*

Mill .... *Dugoob*

Cooking pot .... *Suwhere*

Basket .... *Pa-nyeh*

Seasonings

Pepper ……………………………………………………… *Kani*

Salt ……………………………………………………….. *Ho-rom*

Miscellaneous

Cloth ……………………………………………………… *Piece*

Drinking glass …….…………………………………… *Goblet*

Matches …………………………………………….. *Almet*

Oil ………………………………………………………… *Dew*

Peanut butter …….………………………………… *Deggeh*

Rice …………………………………………………….. *Chĕp*

Rope ……………………………………………….….. *Boom*

Soap ……………………………………………………… *Sabu*

Water ……………………………………….…………. *Ndoh*

Shopping – Key Phrases

Sell me ……………………………………………… *Jaima*

How much? …………………………………… *Nyaata?*

How much for this? ……………………… *Lee nyaata la?*

How much for the tomatoes?……..*Tamateh yi nyaata la?*

How much for these shoes? ………… *Dalla-yee nyaata la?*

Do you take credit cards? …….. Digga nongu credit card?

Where is the ATM? ………………….. Fanla ATM bee nekka?

Where do I buy a calling card?...........*Fanlai gende kartu-telephone?*

Where do I buy a cell phone?.... *Fanlai gende telephone?*

Where do I buy shoes? .... *Fanlai gende dalla?*

Where do I buy clothes? ....*Fanlai gende yearey*

Do you have WiFi/internet? .... *Amga WiFi/internet?*

I want to buy ……………….………………… *Dema buga jenda*

Sell me 2 lbs. of meat (1 kilo) ....*Jaima nyarri kilo yapa*

Sell me 1 lb. of meat (1/2 kilo)... *Jaima bena leebarr yapa*

I wish to pay my bill ……………....................…… *Dema buga fai*

15. Money

5 cents ………………………………………. *Jurome dereum*

One dollar ………………………………………….. *Tehmerr*

10 cents ……………………………………….... *Fuki dereum*

10 dollars ……………………………………………… *Junee*

20 cents ………………………………………. *Nyarr fuke*

16. Days

Sunday .... *Dimas*

Monday .... *Londi*

Tuesday ....*Tarlarta*

Wednesday .... *Alarba*

Thursday .... *Al-hamess*

Friday .... *Arjuma*

Saturday .... *Samdi*

17. Numbers

1.. *Bena*

2... *Nyarr*

3... *Nyaeta*

4... *Nyenta*

5.. *Jurom*

6.. *Jurom bena*

7.. *Jurom nyarr*

8... *Jurom nyaeta*

9... *Jurom nyenta*

10.. *Fukah*

11... *Fukaak bena*

12.. *Fukaak nyarr*

13...*Fukaak nyaeta*

14...*Fukaak nyenta*

15.. *Fukaak jurom*

16... *Fukaak jurom bena*

17.. *Fukaak juom nyarr*

18.. *Fukaak jurom nyaeta*

19.. *Fukaak jurom nyenta*

20.. *Nyarr fuka*

21 etc. .... *Nyarr fukaak bena*

30.. *Nyaeta fuka*

31 etc. .... *Nyaeta fukaak bena*

40.. *Nyenta fuka*

50.. *Jurom fuka*

60.. *Jurom bena fuka*

70.. *Jurom nyarr fuka*

80.. *Jurom nyaeta fuka*

90.. *Jurom nyenta fuka*

100.. *Tehmerr*

200.. *Nyarr tehmerr*

300.. *Nyaeta tehmerr*

400.. *Nyenta tehmerr*

18.Time Words

Today..*Tye*

Tomorrow .... *Elek*

Day after tomorrow ….....…............…….. *Ganaw elek*

Yesterday …….....………………………….... *Demba*

Day before yesterday …..…............…… *Borka demba*

The day …….....………………………….…… *Besbi*

Month ……….....…………………………….… *Wear*

Year …….....……………………………...….. *At*

Morning …………….....……………………… *Suba*

Later ……….....………………………..…… Chicanum

Afternoon …………….....…………………… *Bechek*

Evening …………….....……………………… Ngone

Night ……….....……………………………… *Gudee*

Week ……….....……………………………… *Besboba*

Early morning …………….....……………….. *Suba tel*

Noon …………….....………………………... *Dighee bechek*

Midnight …………….....…………………..... *Dighee gudi*

Today morning …………….....……………… *Tye chi suba*

Yesterday morning …..….....………….…… *Demba chi suba*

Tomorrow morning …..…...............…….… *Elek chi suba*

For the meantime .... *Bala ngoom*

Before evening .... *Bala ngone*

19. Exercise

Person A: How old are you
N'yata at nga am?

Person B: I am 20 years old
Nyarr fuki at la am

Person A: How long have you been here?
Kan- nga fi neck?

Person B: I have been here for 3 years
Neck nahfee nyaeta at
(1 year – *Bena at;* 2 years – *Nyarr at*)

20. Colors

White ....*Weh*

Black ....*Nyule*

Red ....*Honk*

Green ....*Werta*

Yellow ....*Neteh*

Brown ....*Sokola*

Blue ....*Bluh*

Orange ....Orange

Violet ....Veolay

I want a piece of green cloth ....*Piece bu werta la buga*

The book is black ....*Tereh bi defa nyule*

Give me the red hat ....*Johma bahana bu honk*

I want the white
 piece of paper ....D*erma buga kayit bu weh*

21. Verb Exercise

Your mouth...*Sa ghemen*

To borrow..ahball

Borrower..Abu kat

I borrowed a dress from Pam ...... Abu na yeareh chi Pam

To arrive ....Nyoh

I will arrive in NY today ....Deena nyoh NY tai

To need ....Sohula

I need you ....Sohula nala

I need to go to the bathroom ....Sohula na dem toilet

To go...Dem

To go together ....Nanu ahnd

To protect ....Are

Protection ....Karongay

 I need protection ....Dama sohula karongay

To judge.. Ahtay

Judge .... Ahtay Kat

To excuse..Balleh

Excuse me...Ballma

To cancel..Forma

I cancel my meeting...................... Forma na suma ndajay

To bend...Lem

Bend your leg...............................Lemal sa tank

To boil...Bahall

His hand..*Lohom*

They boiled the eggs ....Nyom bahall nanu nan

To run...Dau

Runner..Dau kat

To run after him.......................................Dau chi ghenau

22. Vocabulary

Afternoon snack... *Njogonal*

Aunt... *Yumpañ*

Bad... *Bon*

Beautiful... Ra*fet*

Bed.. *Lall*

Bird .... Pee*cha*

Book... *Tehree*

Breakfast...Ndekee

Calabash.. *Leket*

Carpet .... *Basang*

Cow.. *Nak*

Cup .... *Kass*

Curtain .... *Reedo*

Doctor.. Doctor

Dog.. *Hatch*

Door...*Bunta*

Emergency ....*Urgence*

Evening meal... *Rerr*

Eye.. *Butt*

Father... *Bai*

Fence... *Saket*

Fire.. *Safara*

Fowl.. *Ganaar*

Food... *Nyum*

Goat... *Bei*

Good.. *Bakh*

Grandfather..*Mam bu goor*

Grandmother…..……………………………*Mam bu jegaen*

Hair…………………………………………………… *Kawarr*

Hand……………………………………………………. *Loho*

Head…………………………………………………….. *Bopah*

House………………………………………………………*Kerr*

I don't know…………………………………………….*Haw ma*

It is beautiful…………………………………….. *Defa rafet*

It is enough………………………………………….. *Doyna*

It is ready (I'm ready)…………………………….. *Perehna*

It is too bad…………………………………….. *Bonna torop*

It is too much……………………………………… *Defa bari*

Kaftan……………………………………………….. *Khaftan*

Knife………………………………………………….. *Pakah*

Lamp………………………………………………….. *Lampa*

Lighter………………………………………………*Lampi battri*

Long trousers…………………………………*Tubeyd bu guda*

Lunch………………………………………………… *Ayn*

Medicine ………………………………………………… Garab

Mother………………………………………………… *Yai*

Money……………………………………………….. *Khalis*

Name……………………………………………………. *Turr*

Nothing... *Darra*

Nurse ....Doctor

Pants...Pantalom

Paper... *Kayit*

Pen...*Bic*

Person...*Nit*

Plate... *Plot*

Pump... *Pompeh*

Purse... *Calpeh*

Rag... *Sagarr*

Razor... *Lanset*

Road... *Yonn*

Sand... *Sooff*

Sheep... *Harr*

Shirt...Samiss

Shorts... *Tubeyd bu gata*

Spoon... *Kuddu*

Table... *Tahbul*

Taxi... *Taxi*

Tree...*Garab*

Umbrella...Parasol

Uncle……………………………………………..…….. *Ni jai*

Underwear………………………………………..…*Ghensor*

Watch……………………………………….…… *Montarr loho*

Water pot……………………………………..…. *Potoo'ndal*

Window……………………………………………….. *Parlanterr*

Woman's skirt ……………………………………….…*Mbalan*

23. Exercise

Come let's eat rice ……………………………*Kai lekah chep*

Come let's go home …………………………… *Kai nyeebee*

You are a white man ……………………………*Yow tubab nga*

You are kind …………………………………*Yow danga bah*

You are a coward ………………………………*Yow danga ragal*

You are clean ………………………… *Yow Jow danga set*

You are brave …………………………… *Yow danga jambaray*

You are female ……………………………… *Yow jeegan nga*

You are male ……………………………… *Yow gorr nga*

You are an old man ……………………………… *Yow maget nga*

You are a teacher ……………………… *Yow jangalehkat nga*

You are a driver ……………………………… *Yow Soforr nga*

You are a businessman …………………………… *Yow jula nga*

You are a cook ……………………………… *Yow tourga kat nga*

Myself, head ....*Bopah*

I am, myself ....*Mann mai suma bopah*

You are, yourself .... *Yow yai sa bopah*

Where is my mother? ....*Ana suma yai?*

Have you seen my husband? ....*Gisilo suma jekerr?*

I have no money today ....*Amuma halis tye*

Wait until tomorrow ....*Haral elek*

Wait for me here ....*Harma fi*

What is paining you? ....*Lula meti?*

I like you ....*Buganala*

Who tells you? ....*Kula ko wah?*

I know it for myself ....*Ma ko hamal suma bopah*

Can you speak Wolof? ....*Mungai laka Wolof?*

Yes, I can speak a little Wolof .....*Wau munai laka Wolof-*

tudee

No, I cannot speak Wolof ......*Dedet, munuma laka Wolof*

Can you speak English? ....*Mungai laka Angaleh?*

Can you speak French? ....*Mungai laka Faranseh?*

Can you cook? ....*Mungai torga?*

Can you pound? ....*Mungai wall?*

Can you write? ....*Mungai binda?*

Yes, I can ....*Wau, muna*

Yes, I can do everything ....*Wau muna lep*

No, I cannot ....*Dedet munuma*

Do you know John? ....*Kham nga John?*

Yes I know John ....*Wau kham na John*

I like it very much ....*Bugana ko torop*

I don't like it ....*Bugu-mako*

I will call you ....*Deena la telephonay*

I hear it ....*Dega na*

Everybody ....*Nyep*

I am American ....*Mann American la*

Do you understand? ....*Degan-nga*

I understand, I know ....*Hamna*

I don't know, I don't understand ....*Ha mo ma*

I am tired ....*Dema sonna*

I am hungry ....*Dema hiff*

I am sleepy ....*Dema gomantu*

I am feeling cold ....*Dema le-eu*

He is going to the Mosque ....*Defai dem si jumah bee*

He is coming ....*Munghee nyow*

It is much ....*Defa bari torop*

It is not much ....*Bari wut*

The rain is coming ....*Taw banghee nyow*

The sun is very warm ....*Najbee dafatanga*

The shadow is cold ....*Kerrghee defaseda*

You like me ....*Bungangama*

We like you very much ....*Buganen la torop*

Very much ....*Torop*

Don't do that .... *Bul def lolu*

Don't say that .... *Bul wah lolu*

I will give you .... *Dina la joh*

You will give me .... *Dingmaa joh*

Places To Visit
In
Senegal

PLACES TO VISIT

GOREE ISLAND – Dakar

Goree Island was once a departure point for millions of Africans who were forced into slavery and transported to the Americas. Visit the house where they were kept before departure. Visit The Historical Museum, and the old church.

PINK LAKE - Dakar

The mysterious rose-colored body of water, the Pink Lake. Experience floating in the lake while reading the newspaper. Enjoy a breathtaking adventurous ride to the Atlantic Ocean over the sand dunes in a 4x4. Visit the Fulani village and experience the everyday life of the people.

DJOUDJ NATIONAL BIRD SANCTUARY – St.Louis

It lies on the southeast banks of the River Senegal. It provides a range of wetland habitats which prove very popular with migrating birds. Many of which have just crossed the Sahara. Of almost 400 species of birds, the most visible are pelicans and flamingos. A wide range of wildlife also inhabit the park which is designated a world heritage site.

OTHER PLACES TO VISIT WHILE IN THE CITY OF DAKAR

The Sally Resort

The Saloum Island

The Bandja Resort

The Kedougou Park

Casamance Region

The Soumbedioun Craft Market

The Sea Plaza Mall

The Flower Kermel Market

The Sandaga Market

The Independence Square

The Presidential Place

The Almadie Residential Place

The Grand Mosque of Dakar

The IFAN Museum

The Cheikh Anta Diop University

The Holy City of Touba

TOUR INFORMATION

DA'AFRICAN VILLAGE ORGANIZES TOURS TO WEST AFRICA, SENEGAL, GAMBIA, AND GHANA EVERY OTHER MONTH, YEAR ROUND. FOR MORE INFORMATION PLEASE CONTACT:

DA' AFRICAN VILLAGE

Website: www.daafricanvillage.com

Email: daafricanvillage@gmail.com

Office: (877) 203-5089

"Be on Wings"

with the Da' African Village Travel and Tours

ABOUT THE AUTHOR

Talking Wolof with Da' African Village by Serigne "Mara" Diakhate was inspired by many years of serving as a tour guide leading thousands of people from the United States and Europe through his homeland of Senegal and other countries of West Africa including Gambia, Mali, Mauritania, Ghana and Guinea. He has worked with the largest travel agencies, and is well known in the travel and tourism industry. He has guided celebrities such as Serena Williams, Jessie Jackson, Lauryn Hill, Ky-Mani Marley, Jimmy Cliff and many more. It was during this time that Mara realized the need to create a comprehensive book that will help those traveling abroad communicate more effectively with the people in West Africa.

Serigne" Mara" Diakhate is a native of Dakar, Senegal, and currently resides in Los Angeles, California. He is a world traveler, entrepreneur, and Pan Africanist. Mara is also the CEO and founder of Da' African Village which serves as "A bridge of togetherness" between the United States and Africa. His mission is to share the rich culture and traditions of West Africa with the rest of the world. He believes, "if a person does not know where he comes from, then he does not know where he is going." This is why educating others by equipping them with the knowledge of the history, culture, and language of West Africa has become a part of his life's work.

54751278R00035

Made in the USA
Lexington, KY
27 August 2016